Just for Laughs

TERRIBLY TRICKY TONGUE TWISTERS

Julia Garstecki

BLACK
RABBIT
BOOKS

Hi Jinx is published by Black Rabbit Books
P.O. Box 3263, Mankato, Minnesota, 56002.
www.blackrabbitbooks.com
Copyright © 2018 Black Rabbit Books

Marysa Storm, editor; Michael Sellner, designer;
Omay Ayres, photo researcher

Names: Garstecki, Julia, author.
Title: Terribly tricky tongue twisters / by Julia Garstecki.
Description: Mankato, Minnesota : Black Rabbit Books,
[2018] | Series: Hi jinx. Just for laughs |
Includes bibliographical references and index.
Identifiers: LCCN 2017007253 (print) |
LCCN 2017024148 (ebook) | ISBN
9781680723618 (e-book) |
ISBN 9781680723311 (library binding)
Subjects: LCSH: Tongue twisters–Juvenile
literature. Classification: LCC PN6371.5
(ebook) | LCC PN6371.5 .G37 2018 (print) |
DDC 818/.602–dc23LC record available
at https://lccn.loc.gov/2017007253

Printed in the United States. 10/17

Image Credits

iStock: memoangeles, Cover (goggles), 6–7 (goggles), 23
(goggles); Mikesilent, 15 (mice and peas); Shutterstock:
advent, 10 (shoe, gum); Aga Es, 9 (grapes); akarakingdoms,
5 (dog l); anfisa focusova, 4 (bkgd); Angeliki Vel, 5 (grass);
AntiMartina, 6 (cloud); argus, 15 (bkgd); balabolka, 15 (NY
graphic); blambca, 20 (tongue); Christos Georghiou, 4 (torn ppr),
18 (watch's beard, hair); Chubarov Alexandr, 8 (boots); dedMazay,
8 (turtles); Dmitry Natashin, 2–3, 21 (tongue); Fun Way Illustration, 1
(twister); Graphics RF, 19 (clouds, bolts); Ilya Chalyuk, 5 (marker stroke),
6, (marker stroke), 14 (marker stroke), 18 (marker stroke), 20 (marker
stroke); Incomible, 17 (price tags); IQ Advertising, 14 (mouse); John T
Takai, 8 (coaster); Katrina.Happy, 17 (fish); Kozhadub Sergei, 17 (clam, sand,
wood); Lorelyn Medina, Cover (water), 6–7 (water), 14–15, 17 (coconut),
18 (watch); Mangm srisukh stock photo, 19 (bkgd); Marina BH, 16–17
(woman baking); Memo Angeles, Cover (swans), 4 (wolf), 6–7 (swans), 13
(boy), 17 (snail), 23 (swan); Natykach Nataliia, 13 (PB, bread); Oleksandr
Slobodskyi, 12 (dog); Pasko Maksim, Back Cover (top), 12 (top), 19 (bottom),
23 (top), 24; MicroOne, 17 (shells); Pitju, 9 (curl), 21 (curl); RJC Cartoons,
13 (PB's face); RomanYa, 3, 8–9; Ron Leishman, 1 (kids), 10 (man), 18 (bttm);
schwarzhana, 6 (ballon); Simakova Elena, 12 (grass); S K Chavan, 18 (bowtie);
SuslO, 10 (bubbles); TAW4, 6–7 (choc.); Teguh Mujiono, 5 (dog r), 7 (dog);
totallypic, 13 (arrows), 15 (arrows); Vector Tradition SM, Cover (bkgd), Back
Cover (bkgd); Visual Generation, 14 (ant); vonDUCK, 11; wallnarez, 12 (bkgd);
yaistantine, 20 (man); your, 7 (clouds) Every effort has been made to contact
copyright holders for material reproduced in this book. Any omissions will
be rectified in subsequent printings if notice is given to the publisher.

CONTENTS

Chapter 1
Tricky, Troubling Tongue Twisters

Tongue twisters are phrases that trip the tongue. The faster you say them, the sillier they sound. But they also help mouths get ready to move with ease. Presenting a play about princesses and porcupines? A tongue twister will help you prepare! Get ready to laugh with these tongue-tangling twisters!

Chapter 2

Level One

Warm up your mouth with these easy tongue twisters.

The brilliant blue balloon blew back.

thirty thick **thistles**

brownie
batter
blizzard

The peppy
puppy piddled.

Seven silver swans
swam swiftly.

7

Seven silly sisters
sell shiny shoes.

Tracy tries treating
tangled turtles.

These are short but sticky! Repeat them quickly for **maximum** twisting!

BUBBLE BOBBLE

Sam's sauce shop

gooey shoe glue

Fun Fact

There is an international tongue twister contest that happens every year. Contestants compete in English.

Kick sticky bricks.

leather weathered
wetter weather

black backpack

Pete's bitter peanut butter

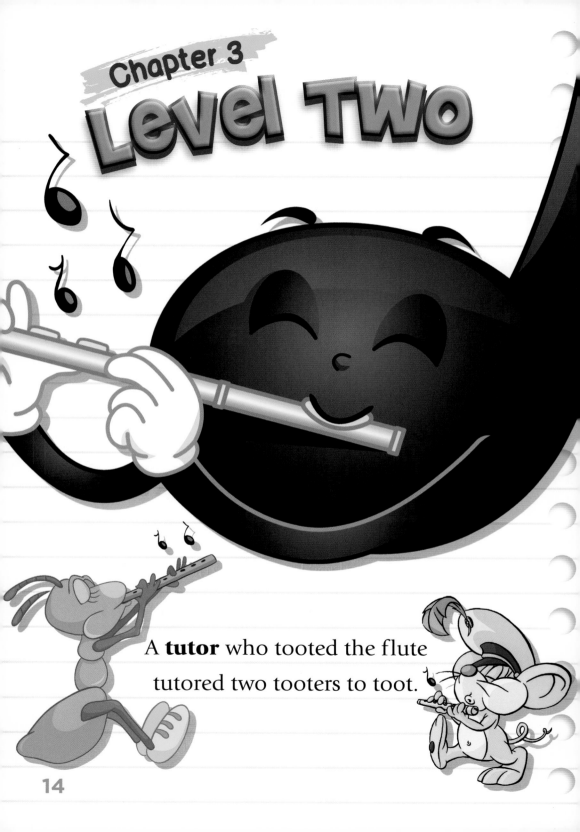

Chapter 3
Level Two

A **tutor** who tooted the flute
tutored two tooters to toot.

a quick-witted **critic**

Please pass the peas.

Here are some classic tongue twisters.

Betty Botter bought some butter.
"But," she said, "this butter's bitter.
If I bake this bitter butter, it will make my batter bitter.
But a bit of better butter would make my batter better."
So Betty Botter bought a bit of better butter.

She sells seashells by the seashore.

Fun Fact
Tongue twisters come in all languages. A Spanish tongue twister is "Como poco coco como, poco coco compro." It means "Since I eat little coconut, little coconut I buy."

These might be short, but they'll tangle your tongue!

Irish wristwatch

Sherry shares short shirts.

flash message

Fun Fact

According to a record book, one tongue twister is harder than any other. It is "The sixth sick **sheikh's** sixth sheep's sick."

Chapter 5
Get in on the Hi Jinx

Tongue twisters are not just for fun. They are used by **newscasters** and actors. They help strengthen muscles used during speaking. If you have to give a presentation, warm up with a tongue twister. It will help you speak clearly.

Take It One Step More

1. Tongue twisters have been around for a long time. Why do you think people started saying them?

2. Try writing your own tongue twister. List words that begin with the same letter. Combine them to make a tricky twister.

3. Which twisters were the hardest for you? Why do you think they were harder than others?

GLOSSARY

critic (KRIT-ik)—a person who makes or gives a judgment of the value, worth, beauty, or excellence of something

international (in-tur-NASH-uh-nuhl)—including more than one nation

maximum (MAK-suh-muhm)—the highest number or amount that is possible or allowed

newscaster (NOOZ-kas-ter)—someone who presents the news on a radio or TV program

sheikh (SHEEK)—an Arab chief, ruler, or prince

thistle (THIS-uhl)—a wild plant that has sharp points on its leaves and purple, yellow, or white flowers

tutor (TOO-ter)—a teacher who works with one student

unique (yoo-NEEK)—very special or unusual

BOOKS

Elliott, Rob. *Laugh-Out-Loud Awesome Jokes for Kids.* Laugh-Out-Loud Jokes for Kids. New York: HarperCollins, 2017.

Gowsell-Pattison, Rosie. *Just Joking 5: 300 Hilarious Jokes about Everything, Including Tongue Twisters, Riddles, and More!* Washington, D.C.: National Geographic, 2014.

Rice, Dona Herweck. *Communicate!: Tongue Twisters.* Time for Kids. Huntington Beach, CA: Teacher Created Materials, 2017.

WEBSITES

Funny Tongue Twisters
americanfolklore.net/folklore/2010/07/funny_tongue_twisters.html

Tongue-Twisters
www.englishclub.com/pronunciation/tongue-twisters.htm

Tongue Twisters for Kids
www.brownielocks.com/tonguetwisters.html

INDEX